THE SPY AT JACOB'S LADDER

AND OTHER BIBLE STORIES FROM THE INSIDE OUT

Lindsay Hardin Freeman
with Len Freeman, Story Collaborator
Illustrations by Paul Shaffer

Forward Movement
Cincinnati, Ohio

© 2018 Forward Movement

ISBN 978-088028-459-2

Printed in the USA

Forward
Movement
inspire disciples. empower evangelists.

THE SPY AT JACOB'S LADDER

AND OTHER BIBLE STORIES FROM THE INSIDE OUT

Lindsay Hardin Freeman

august 2018

Dedicated to Len Freeman,
companion and soul mate

CONTENTS

INTRODUCTION

This book and its companion, *The Spy on Noah's Ark,* offer an experience of reading the Bible in a new way that is up close and personal. You will hear from unlikely sources—a rock, a donkey, a water jug, and more—as they share what it was like to witness some of the Bible's most important moments.

Think of these sources as private investigators, spies, if you will. Up until now, they've been quiet, keeping their thoughts to themselves. After all, donkeys can't talk—or can they? Here—and in the Old Testament—one does!

As you read these stories and think about what it was like to live in biblical times, think of yourself as a spy. What conversations do you hear? What do you see? What do you notice as you look around?

If you are a parent, grandparent, or teacher, bless you for seeking out new ways to share God's word with your young ones. Too often the Bible is dismissed because it seems intimidating or irrelevant. But perhaps that is because we approach it with only a one-dimensional part of ourselves—our adult side. Somewhere we have lost our ability to play, imagine, and simply believe—characteristics that Jesus so values in children.

Walk with the spies through these stories and gain a new perspective into God's world. Hear from rocks and trees and fishing boats and sewing needles. Celebrate the ways in which creation is much deeper and more surprising than we will ever fully understand. Perhaps most important of all, let yourself and those you love play inside these stories. Find joy in them. *Find God in them.*

On this day, the LORD has acted; we will rejoice and be glad in it (Psalm 118:24).

Lindsay Hardin Freeman

ACKNOWLEDGEMENTS

While it may look like writing is a solitary experience, no good writer writes alone—such is clearly the case here. I am deeply grateful for all those who have supported me in helping this book come to life.

For the staff and leadership of Forward Movement, especially Richelle Thompson and Scott Gunn, and for their commitment to sharing God's Word;

For editor Rachel Jones, for her deep faith, late-night support, and joy in God's Word;

For artist Paul Shaffer, who transforms printed words into beautiful living creatures, full of grace and spirit;

For research companions Susan Webster and Joyce White, who never tire of new biblical insights and the hard work needed to discover them;

For the Minnesota faith communities of St. Nicholas, Richfield; St. David's, Minnetonka; and Trinity Church, Excelsior; and for St. Jude's Episcopal Church in Ocean View, Hawaii;

For joyful support from Cindy Hilger, Anne Larner, Barbara Dundon, Mary Beth Farrell, Cordelia Burt, and Laura Anderson;

For Michelle Holtze, who now helps from heaven;

For sons Jeffrey and David Freeman, for their enthusiasm, love, and humorous insight;

And for husband Len Freeman, whose soul resounds throughout this book as color commentator and finish carpenter. He is particularly responsible for the voices of Gordy the Fishing Boat and the Ark of the Covenant.

SARAH'S WILD LAUGHTER
As Told by the Oak of Mamre

Some say that I am dead. As dead as the papery shell a butterfly leaves behind when it flies free. As dead as an autumn-burnished leaf, slipped loose from its mother tree. But I will tell you a secret: Once somebody or something is alive in God's creation, even if our bodies slip away, we are still alive, held tight by God's love. God loves everything that has been made and never lets any of us go.

To this day, my body stands on the very spot where I heard an astounding conversation thousands of years ago. I am an oak tree, called the Oak of Mamre (pronounced Mom-Ray). A small group of us trees stood strong back then, when an old man named Abraham and his wife Sarah lived near us, camping out in the desert with their family, servants, and sheep. I am the only one left now.

The desert was a lonely place. And Sarah was one sad woman. One night when she and Abraham were out for a walk under the stars, I could see her lean against him, wiping her tears away.

I knew why she was crying. She was almost ninety years old and didn't have any children. In those days, having children meant everything.

Oh, how I wanted to comfort her. I rustled my leaves and held my branches out wide, hoping she might think the grassy spot under me would be a good place to rest.

She didn't look my way. But I could feel my trunk stand straighter as Abraham glanced in my direction.

"Come with me, dear," he said to Sarah. "Come sit with me under this beautiful tree."

And they did, nestling against me. Sarah tried to stop the tears running down her cheeks, but, after a while, she gave in to them.

"God promised us that we would have children," cried Sarah. "I don't understand how he could go back on his word."

"My love, we must have faith," Abraham said. Leaning into me and wrapping his arms around Sarah, he reminded her of the promises God made some twenty-five years before: that they would have land of their own—God called it a land flowing with milk and honey—and that they would have as many descendants as there were stars in the sky. They had been trekking through deserts and wilderness ever since.

I wish I could tell you Sarah felt joyful after hearing Abraham's words, or even confident. But she just grew quiet.

When they stood to leave, Sarah steadied herself on my trunk. I stood even taller then, standing as strong as I could for her. Hand in hand, Abraham and Sarah walked back to their tent.

The next afternoon brought the event that I will never forget—the one that changed history.

Abraham was staying cool, sitting at the door of his tent, as he often did during the heat of the day. Sarah was taking a nap. Suddenly, three men seemed to grow out of the desert sand. They hadn't been there a minute ago, when I had glanced off to the west. But they were there now and heading straight for the old man.

Desert hospitality demands that you share the best food and drink that you have with guests, even on the spur of the moment. And Abraham did just that, asking Sarah to make stew for dinner.

Not knowing who the men were, she placed her ear against the tent wall to hear their conversation while she made dinner. She knew, as did I, that people don't just pop up out of sand and thin air. I could almost hear her questions: *Who are these people? Why are they there? Where did they come from?*

I was just as curious. Hunching down, I held my limbs still so there would be no rustling to drown out their voices.

"When we come back in a year, Sarah will have given birth to a son," said one of the three visitors.

Abraham's mouth fell open. And on the other side of the tent, Sarah started to laugh to herself.

The same person who had shared the stunning news looked at Abraham. "Why is your wife laughing?"

Abraham came around the tent wall to find her, asking, "Why did you laugh?"

Oops! Sarah knew it was impolite to eavesdrop—and even worse to be caught laughing at visitors!

"I did not laugh," Sarah fibbed.

"Yes, you did!"

Well, I knew why Sarah had laughed. You probably do too. Sarah was ninety years old, and ninety-year-old women don't have babies! Especially after following very old husbands around in the wilderness for years and years.

As the strange visitors walked away, the one who told Abraham about Sarah's baby brushed his hand against my trunk. "You are a beautiful tree," he whispered. "I have loved you since the day I made you."

What? And then I knew. The three visitors weren't people. Two of them were angels, and one—the One who had spoken to Abraham and to me—was actually God!

Imagine that: God, the maker of all things, right there in front of me!

🕯 🕯 🕯

A year later, Sarah did in fact give birth to a son. And she was so happy that she named him Isaac, which means *he will laugh*. In the years following Isaac's birth, I heard plenty of joy and laughter come from their tent.

After this special family moved on, the night winds told me that Abraham and Sarah had many grandchildren and great-grandchildren, just like God promised. Their descendants came to be known as the children of Israel, and they loved God very much.

🕯 🕯 🕯

Note:

The Oak of Mamre, also called the Oak of Abraham, is said to mark the spot where the angels visited Sarah and Abraham. Located 1.2 miles southwest of Mamre,

 *near Hebron, it has been declared officially dead, but parts of its ancient trunk are said to still remain.*

QUESTIONS TO CONSIDER
YOUNGER READERS

What do you think it would feel like to wander in the desert for years and years, not exactly sure where you were going?

Abraham and Sarah listened carefully for God's voice. When have you listened for God's voice? What did you hear?

Sarah wanted a baby more than anything. Have you ever wanted something so badly? Did you talk with God about it? What did you learn from the conversation?

Look at the sky tonight. What did it mean when God told Abraham that he and Sarah would have as many descendants as there were stars in the sky?

OLDER READERS

Following God's voice was the cornerstone of faith for Abraham and Sarah. They were told that they would have as many descendants as there are stars in the sky (Genesis 26:4). Yet Sarah, approaching ninety, was still childless. What messages might the Holy Spirit be communicating through this story?

Sarah and Abraham must have significantly downsized in order to begin their great adventure at ages 65 and 80. Is there anything you would need to downsize to respond better to God's call?

THE BIBLE STORY

Genesis 18:1-15. The LORD appeared to Abraham by the oaks of Mamre, as he sat at the entrance of his tent in the heat of the day. He looked up and saw three men standing near him. When he saw them, he ran from the tent entrance to meet them, and bowed down to the ground. He said, "My lord, if I find favor with you, do not pass by your servant. Let a little water be brought, and wash your feet, and rest yourselves under the tree. Let me bring a little bread, that you may refresh yourselves, and after that you may pass on—since you have come to your servant." So they said, "Do as you have said." And Abraham hastened into the tent to Sarah, and said, "Make ready quickly three measures of choice flour, knead it, and make cakes." Abraham ran to the herd, and took a calf, tender and good, and gave it to the servant, who hastened to prepare it. Then he took curds and milk and the calf that he had prepared, and set it before them; and he stood by them under the tree while they ate.

They said to him, "Where is your wife Sarah?" And he said, "There, in the tent." Then one said, "I will surely return to you in due season, and your wife Sarah shall have a son." And Sarah was listening at the tent entrance behind him. Now Abraham and Sarah were old, advanced in age; it had ceased to be with Sarah after the manner of women. So Sarah laughed to herself, saying, "After I have grown old, and my husband is old, shall I have pleasure?" The LORD said to Abraham, "Why did Sarah laugh, and say, 'Shall I indeed bear a child, now that I am old?' Is anything too wonderful for the LORD? At the set time I will return to you, in due season, and Sarah shall have a son." But Sarah denied, saying, "I did not laugh"; for she was afraid. He said, "Oh yes, you did laugh."

JACOB: ANGELS, LADDERS, AND BOTHERSOME BROTHERS
As Told by the Pillow Rock

I am a rock: big, flat, gray, and proud. You might think I'm exceptionally boring. But you have no idea what I saw one night, out in the wilderness that came to be known as Bethel.

I had just settled down for the evening. I did what I have always done: I sat there, unmoving, like I had done for thousands of years. I yearned for someone to come along and kick me, so I could get a new place to sit for the next century! (Don't worry. Kicks don't hurt rocks.)

Just as I was trying to drop off to sleep, a wild-eyed man burst out from behind a clump of bushes. Slight of frame and red of face, he dropped to his knees about three feet in front of me.

"Save me, God, save me! Don't let him kill me!!"

I looked around, without moving, as we rocks do. No one was chasing him. Who was he afraid of?

"I shouldn't have done it," he said. "Now I'm really in trouble."

Curious, I sent out an emergency request along the ROCK (Rock Ordering Crucial Knowledge) Network. Boulder to stone to pebble, the question was passed: *Who is this guy? What is he running from?*

The stranger paced in circles around me.

"I shouldn't have stolen Esau's birthright! I shouldn't have lied about who I am! No wonder Esau wants to kill me!"

Who was Esau? And what if he suddenly appeared? Worry mounted within me like a rogue wave. *What if this Esau guy showed up? What if he took out his anger by throwing and breaking me into a thousand pieces?*

Panic attack! Just as I was losing my grip, word started coming back from my granite and basalt friends, the ROCK Network. In language that had been hammered out over millions of years, they told me the story.

The scared man who was circling around me was Jacob. Esau was his brother. Esau was as hairy and wild as Jacob was slender and pale. Although they were twins, they were as different as night and day. Esau spent a lot of time outdoors, hunting and fishing. Jacob was an inside kind of guy who liked to cook vegetables and think deep thoughts.

Esau had been born just minutes before Jacob. That was a big deal, for it meant that Esau was entitled to most of his family's inheritance. In those days, this was called a birthright. When your father gave you a special birthright blessing, it meant you were in charge of the whole family.

Well, it turns out that Jacob wanted this blessing. He waited patiently for a way to get the birthright blessing (and all the privileges that came with it) for himself. One day, he heard his father Isaac say he would like to eat his favorite food—a savory meat stew—before he died.

"Esau, take your bow and arrow and shoot me a deer," said Isaac. "Then make me some stew, and I'll give you my blessing. You will be in charge."

Esau went out, bow in hand. And then Rebekah, the twin's mother, looked at Jacob, whom she particularly loved.

"Quick, Jacob!" she said. "Go get me a couple of goats. and I will make your father's favorite stew. He will think you are Esau, and then you will get the special blessing!"

"But Esau is hairy, and I am smooth," Jacob said. "Dad will know the difference. What if he touches my bare arms? Or even smells me? You know Esau smells bad sometimes. Dad will know it's not him!"

"I'll take care of that!" ordered Rebekah. "Go find those goats now, or it will be too late."

Jacob found the goats, and Rebekah worked furiously to turn them into the meat stew that Isaac loved.

"Put these goatskins on your arms," she said. "They will make you feel hairy, and your father will think you are Esau."

Then Rebekah gave Jacob a bowl of hot stew.

"Take this to your father now before Esau gets back!"

Hairy and balancing the steaming bowl of stew, Jacob approached his father.

"Here I am, Dad," Jacob said. "I have your favorite stew, and I am ready for your blessing."

"Come over here," said Isaac. "You don't sound like Esau...you sound like Jacob."

Trembling, Jacob walked closer and held out his goatskin-covered arms. Isaac ran his hands up and down them and then smiled.

"Esau, it *is* you," he said. "And because you are who you are, I give you my blessing. Anyone who curses you shall be cursed. Anyone who blesses you shall be blessed. Everyone will bow down before you and do whatever you say."

Breathing a huge sigh of relief, Jacob left the tent. And not a moment too soon, for in walked Esau.

"Dad, I have your stew!"

"Who are you?" Isaac asked, confused.

"I'm Esau, your firstborn, ready for my blessing."

"Oh, no!" said Isaac. "Your brother was just here and tricked me. I have already given him my blessing!"

"Does this mean there's nothing left for me?" asked Esau.

"I can only give you a very small blessing," said Isaac. The special birthright blessing was binding, meaning that Isaac couldn't take it back. "I am so sorry."

"Where is that lying, scheming brother of mine?" shouted Esau. "I will break every bone in his small pale body! I will kill him for doing this to me!"

🔑 🔑 🔑

Ah...what a story! Now I understood why Jacob was pacing around me like a scared rabbit, waiting to be roasted over a fire and devoured. He knew he had done something wrong, and he was afraid of his brother coming to hurt him.

But even scared rabbits have to sleep eventually.

Out of all the rocks scattered on the desert floor, he picked me to serve as his pillow. He laid his tear-streaked face on my cool surface and drifted off into a restless sleep.

Then something happened that I have never forgotten: The sky opened up and a ladder gently unfolded, reaching from behind the clouds down to the ground.

Jacob bolted upright. Together, we watched as angels of all colors and sizes danced up and down the ladder, fleet of foot and musical in step. Some shimmered green like wind-swept grass or translucent blue like the ocean; others changed colors and shapes as they moved up and down, up and down.

Suddenly a voice burst forth from the heavens: strong, commanding, sure.

"I am the God of Abraham and Isaac, of Sarah and Rebekah! All this land—to the north and south and east and west—I will give to you and your children and grandchildren. I will stay with you; I will protect you wherever you go. I will bring you back to this very ground."

Wow! In all of my years of desert life, I had never heard or seen anything like this. Talk about love coming right from the top.

"God is in this place!" whispered Jacob. "And I didn't even know...This is incredible. Wonderful. Holy. This is God's house. This *is* the Gate of Heaven!"

🔑 🔑 🔑

This part of the story was hard for me to understand. Jacob had tricked his brother and was running away. It was his fault, but somehow God was there for Jacob. God forgave Jacob and was teaching him how to be a good man. Jacob ended up spending many years in a distant land. He started his own family and learned how to love.

But you cannot stay away from brothers forever. And one day, it was time for Jacob to go back.

God bless Esau, who also had grown into a wiser man. When he heard that Jacob was headed home, he went out, met his twin on the road and, just like God, forgave him.

Some say the angels that Jacob saw were just a dream. But I know better. Sometimes God reaches us in our darkest hour and shows us the way ahead.

QUESTIONS TO CONSIDER
YOUNGER READERS

Do you think it was fair for Jacob to steal his brother's blessing? How might he have handled that better?

Have you ever been angry with someone in your family or a close friend? How did you work it out?

How did the angels help Jacob? Why do you think they appeared to him?

Have you ever seen an angel? Have you heard anyone talk about them? Draw a picture of what you think an angel looks like.

The Bible says that angels have special jobs in heaven and on earth. Some are messengers. Others praise God all day long. Some fight heavenly battles. Some have names, like Gabriel. There are thousands of them, all working for God. What would you say to an angel? How might you call on angels to help you?

OLDER READERS

Jacob and his mother were deceptive in arranging for him to get his father's blessing. Can such an action be justified? Where is God in this?

Do you believe in angels? Have you ever seen an angel? How might they be present to you without your even knowing it?

Throughout the Bible, God seems to work through dreams, intuition, and heavenly beings outside of our normal realm of experience. How might you be more open to God's messages and messengers? How might you call upon them to help you in your work?

THE BIBLE STORY

Genesis 28:11-22. [Jacob] came to a certain place and stayed there for the night, because the sun had set. Taking one of the stones of the place, he put it under his head and lay down in that place. And he dreamed that there was a ladder set up on the earth, the top of it reaching to heaven; and the angels of God were ascending and descending on it. And the LORD stood beside him and said, "I am the LORD, the God of Abraham your father and the God of Isaac; the land on which you lie I will give to you and to your offspring; and your offspring shall be like the dust of the earth, and you shall spread abroad to the west and to the east and to the north and to the south; and all the families of the earth shall be blessed in you and in your offspring. Know that I am with you and will keep you wherever you go, and will bring you back to this land; for I will not leave you until I have done what I have promised you." Then Jacob woke from his sleep and said, "Surely the LORD is in this place—and I did not know it!" And he was afraid, and said, "How awesome is this place! This is none other than the house of God, and this is the gate of heaven."

So Jacob rose early in the morning, and he took the stone that he had put under his head and set it up for a pillar and poured oil on the top of it. He called that place Bethel; but the name of the city was Luz at the first. Then Jacob made a vow, saying, "If God will be with me, and will keep me in this way that I go, and will give me bread to eat and clothing to wear, so that I come again to my father's house in peace, then the LORD shall be my God, and this stone, which I have set up for a pillar, shall be God's house; and of all that you give me I will surely give one-tenth to you."

JOSEPH AND ME
As Told by the Coat of Many Colors

People call me "The Coat of Many Colors." I am pretty snazzy, after all, and probably the most famous coat in history.

Picture a rainbow, and then imagine it pouring over your shoulders. I am like that rainbow: flowing and warm, full of color and life and energy. I was made for a seventeen-year old boy named Joseph, who was his father's favorite son.

I knew there was trouble afoot, even from the time that I was being made. I could feel it coming the day that Joseph's father, Israel, came to see the tailor who was piecing me together. Israel had been in the shop before to place the order. Now he wanted to make sure that I was everything he had hoped.

"Make this the most beautiful coat in the world," Israel told the tailor, "for Joseph is the most intelligent, bravest, and best-looking son ever!"

The tailor cringed, his hands clutching my fabric.

"Israel," he said. "You have twelve sons and a beautiful daughter! How can Joseph be the best? Surely he is a fine boy...but your other children are wonderful as well!"

"You are right," Israel said. "Joseph's youngest brother, Benjamin, is a delight as well. He and Joseph have the same mother. Those two boys are my favorites. But the others? Well..."

Yikes! Parents are not supposed to favor one set of children over others. Even I know that. But no one asked me for my opinion. And to be honest, I was pretty busy admiring the process by which my parts were coming together.

Deep purple and red silks. Hand-dyed wool in blues and greens. A soft lining of sheepskin. Yellow and orange swaths of linen, all pieced together with the finest threads.

Wow, I was one fine coat! And Joseph knew it. When Israel first presented me to him, the kid put me on and went prancing about like a day-old colt. All of this bragging and showing off did not sit well with his brothers.

Things turned even worse when Joseph told them about some of his dreams.

"I had a dream about all of you," he said. "I dreamt that we were binding wheat into bundles in the field, and my bundle stood upright and all of yours bowed down to mine."

This is not the kind of thing brothers like to hear. People who have special gifts sometimes need to think twice before they blurt things out.

Within a few days, Joseph unwisely shared even more of his dreams.

"I dreamed that the sun and the moon and eleven stars were bowing down to me!"

This time, even his father Israel was irritated. This is not the kind of thing a father wants to hear.

"What is this?" Israel cried. "Are you saying that your mother and I, and your brothers and sisters, should all bow ourselves to the ground before you!?"

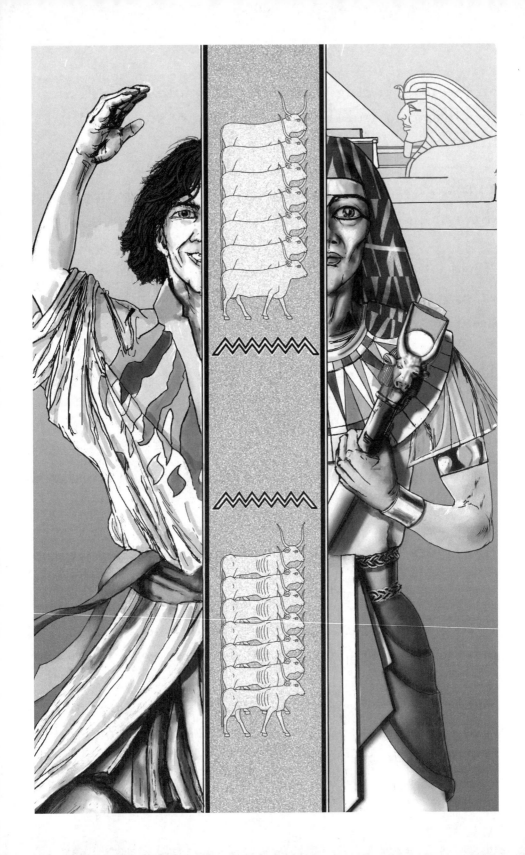

Ouch. I don't think Joseph knew how to answer his father. Most seventeen-year-olds think they are always right. But as it turns out, even though the dreams seemed preposterous, God actually was talking to Joseph through his dreams. God was giving hints of things to come, for Joseph's life would be one of great service to many people and especially to Israel's family. But the boy had some growing up to do first. Unfortunately, that would happen at the hands of his brothers.

One sunny day, when the two youngest boys were at home with their father, the old man called Joseph to his side.

"Your brothers are busy watching our sheep near Shechem," he said. "Go find out how they are doing, and bring me word."

Joseph wrapped me around his shoulders, and he set out for what should have been a routine visit to the fields. Because of my bright colors, his brothers—who were still very angry with him—saw Joseph coming. A dark spirit of jealousy and hatred overcame them.

"There's that dreamer," they muttered. "Let's kill him! Let's take him and throw him into a pit and say a wild beast ate him up!"

One of the brothers, Reuben, tried to protect Joseph. "Shed no blood," he said. "Sure, we can throw him into a pit, but let's not really hurt him."

When Joseph and I arrived, the brothers tore me off his shoulders and threw both of us down into a deep pit filled with jagged rocks and gravel. As we lay there, Joseph bruised and bleeding, we heard the angry voices of the older brothers.

"Get rid of him," growled one. "Let's be done with 'Mister-I'm-SO-Important.'"

"We're better off without him," said another.

Like flames of fire, jealousy and anger danced around the pit, growing hotter by the minute. Then, a brother named Judah came up with a different plan.

"What do we profit if we kill him? Besides, he is our brother, our own flesh and blood," Judah said. Spotting a group of traders in the distance, Judah suggested to the brothers: "We could sell Joseph as a slave!"

Within minutes, Joseph and I were hauled out from the pit. The brothers tore me up and sold Joseph to the slave traders for twenty pieces of silver. I had expected to go with Joseph, but that was not to be…at least for most of me. Joseph was able to hold onto a scrap from one of my beautiful sleeves. That is how I came to know the rest of the story.

I am sad to say that the brothers continued their cowardly lying ways. Shredding me into rags, they dipped me in goat's blood, then brought the pieces home to their father. "This is what we have found."

Israel recognized Joseph's coat. Believing that wild beasts had killed his beloved son, the old man crumpled to the floor of his tent. Weeks of mourning stretched into years.

This is a hard story to tell. But take a breath. It gets better. Trust me.

♟ ♟ ♟

God did not leave Joseph in slavery. The slave traders took Joseph to Egypt, and he went to work in Pharaoh's palace.

Remember those dreams Joseph had as a boy? Sometimes God gives us gifts that save our lives. Being able to talk about and understand dreams was one of Joseph's special gifts.

Deep inside the palace, Pharaoh had been having terrifying dreams. He described the dreams to all the wise men in the country, but no one could tell him what they meant.

And then someone remembered Joseph. He had helped some of the other palace staff understand their dreams, so maybe he could help the Pharaoh. They sent for Joseph, who calmly listened to Pharaoh's dream.

"There I was," said Pharaoh, "standing on the banks of the Nile River. And out of the river came seven fat cows that ate beautiful green grass by the river. And then, out of the same river came seven skinny cows that stood beside the fat cows. And the skinny cows ate up the fat ones!"

Joseph listened carefully.

"The next day I had another dream," continued Pharaoh. "Seven ears of grain, strong and plump, were growing on one stalk. But then, seven thin ears sprouted, blighted by the east wind, and the thin ears swallowed up the seven plump and full ears! What does all this mean?"

Joseph thought for a moment and then answered: "I can tell you exactly what those dreams mean: Egypt will have seven good years of rainfall, where crops will grow well. But then there will be seven years of no rain and no crops. All the food will be gone, and the people will starve unless we take steps to prepare now."

Joseph told Pharaoh to grow as much food as possible in the next seven years and store some of it so that there would be food during the years of famine and drought.

"You will be able to save your people from starving," Joseph said.

From deep in Joseph's pocket where I had been since his brothers sold him into slavery, I marveled at how the ungracious boy had grown into a kind and wise man. And Pharaoh sensed this spirit as well. In fact he promoted Joseph to come and work as a governor, placing him in charge of Egypt's food preparations.

When the famine came in seven years, it dried up not only Egypt but also all of the nearby land, including Canaan, where Joseph's family lived. This is how the people of Israel came to live in Egypt.

On the brink of starvation, Joseph's brothers came to Egypt for help. They didn't know the little brother they had sold into slavery was now in charge of this vast country. When they realized it, they were scared. Joseph would have control over whether they would live or die. What would he do to them?

But Joseph had grown into a wise and good man. After many tears and prayers, Joseph forgave them. "What you meant for evil," he told them, "God used for good."

And isn't that just the way God works in the world? Even a scrap of a once-beautiful coat like me knows that God is always doing more than we could ask or imagine.

QUESTIONS TO CONSIDER
YOUNGER READERS

Joseph wasn't very nice to his brothers, always bragging and acting like he was the best. But his brothers didn't behave well either. Have you ever been mean to your family? Have your family members ever been mean to you? How did you handle it?

Joseph forgave his brothers and arranged for them to come and live near him in Egypt. Have you ever forgiven someone? How did it work out?

Even when Joseph was taken into slavery and was scared, God was with Joseph and took care of him. Think about how God is with you, both in good times and not-so-good times.

OLDER READERS

The story of Joseph is complex. Clearly, teenage Joseph was somewhat arrogant—or at least insensitive—and irritated his family. Once grown, however, he developed into a responsible and inspiring leader. Does Joseph's story ring true with any parts of your own life?

Joseph's brothers sold him into slavery, and after substantial tears and maneuvering, he eventually forgave them. Have you known heartbreak at the hands of family members? How was God present to you during that time? How have you been able to reconcile betrayal or pain?

In Genesis 50:20, Joseph assures his brothers that what they meant for evil, God used for good. Consider the theological ramifications for this idea, both biblically and in your own life.

THE BIBLE STORY

Genesis 37:3-4. Now Israel loved Joseph more than any other of his children, because he was the son of his old age; and he had made him a long robe with sleeves. But when his brothers saw that their father loved him more than all his brothers, they hated him, and could not speak peaceably to him.

For the whole story of Joseph, read Genesis chapters 37-50.

PART THOSE WATERS, MOSES!
As Told by the Staff of Moses

NO!! It couldn't be! WHAT was happening??

One minute I was a shepherd's staff: tall, good-looking, and proud.

The next thing I knew, I was writhing around on the ground in a scaly, creepy, silvery body—a snake's body! Twisting and lunging. Angry. Flicking my out-of-control tongue at everything and everyone. I hissed and spat and was mad, mad, mad.

I'll tell you more about that moment. But the important part is that God was using me to get the attention of my owner Moses. And I can tell you that it worked!

The day started out like any other. We were doing
what shepherds and their helpers do: watching sheep.
Making sure that none got snatched away by lions or
bears or rustlers. Helping the sheep find sweet grass
and clear water. Enjoying the young lambs as they
frolicked on the hillside.

Every so often, I would pull a young lamb back from a
dangerous cliff. Or Moses would stick me in a stream to
see how deep it was before he carried sheep across on
his broad shoulders. I was, of course, on call to fight off
dangerous hyenas—but since we hadn't seen any of those in
many years, I didn't have to act braver than I really was.

Mostly we lived amidst the quiet sounds of sheep and
the simple beauty of the hillsides. So, imagine our shock
when Moses and I stumbled across a bush burning for no
reason—all on its own!

We watched, mesmerized, as the flames roared and sizzled.

"Perhaps it's been struck by lightning!" Moses exclaimed.

Like staffs do, I stiffly shook my head. There had been
no storms that day.

"Perhaps someone came and set it on fire," Moses suggested.

I looked around. We were totally alone. And I hadn't seen any sheep carrying matches.

"Maybe it spontaneously combusted!"

I looked at Moses. Things do not just start burning for no reason at all, and we both knew it.

This was the weirdest fire ever. The flames didn't consume the bush. About ten feet high and eight feet across, they roared and crackled and rumbled like an angry dinosaur, out to destroy everything in its path. But the bush was still there.

Then came a voice, louder than I have ever heard before—or since: "Moses! Moses! Take off your shoes, for you are standing on holy ground! I am the God of your fathers and mothers, the God of Abraham and Sarah, of Isaac and Rebekah, of Jacob, Leah, and Rachel."

Yikes! God was speaking out of the burning bush!

Pulling his cloak over his face, Moses tried to hide.

Hey buddy, I thought. *No use hiding. God knows you're here.*

"Moses," God said, "I have a job for you. I have heard my people crying in Egypt. Their suffering is overwhelming. But they shall be slaves no longer! I have come down to rescue them and to bring them to a good land where they will be free."

Moses knew about God's people in Egypt, for he had grown up there. He had seen God's people work in the hot sun making bricks until they fainted. He'd seen them starved and beaten, treated like rats. Later I would learn that Moses had killed an Egyptian who was beating one of the Israelites. That is why we were out here, tending sheep. Moses had fled to the desert after killing the cruel Egyptian.

"Go back to Egypt and rescue my people," said God. "Tell Pharaoh to let my people go!"

"Who shall I say has sent me?" asked Moses.

"I AM WHO I AM," said God. "Tell them I AM has sent you!"

"But what if Pharaoh doesn't believe me?" Moses asked. "What if Pharaoh doesn't believe that you ordered me to do this, and he kills me instead?"

God thundered: "What is in your hand?"

Oh no. That would be me.

"My staff," said Moses.

"Throw it on the ground!"

And that's when the horrible thing happened. At my very top, I felt a flickering. Buckling out from under me, my stiff staff knees disappeared. Gone were my smooth, hand-rubbed contours. I thrashed around, ravenous for food. Moses' ankles looked tasty. I slithered toward them, my tongue lashing out.

"Moses, reach down and grab that snake by the tail!" commanded the Voice.

And thank God that Moses did. As soon as Moses grabbed me, I transformed back into my sleek, upright self.

"There!" God said. "Do that for Pharaoh, and he will know who sent you!"

No! I screamed inwardly. I would have to do this snake thing again?

39

Moses kept going back and forth with God. I could tell he would rather walk away.

"I am not very good at talking with people," Moses said. "I get nervous, and I stutter. How will I even know what to say when I face Pharaoh?"

Nice try, Moses, I thought. But God wasn't accepting any of Moses' excuses.

"Ah, you are right," said God. "You do have that stuttering problem. I will send your big brother Aaron to go with you. He is a very good talker."

We headed down to Egypt then, the four of us: Moses, Aaron, me, and Aaron's staff. While Moses and Aaron slept, Aaron's staff and I talked late into the night. Somehow, maybe because of my new friend, I found the strength to do what God needed.

We stood in front of Pharaoh—not once, but ten times—all four of us. Moses and Aaron told Pharaoh to release the slaves, to let God's people go. But each time, like a big foot squashing a bug, Pharaoh turned them down flat. God inflicted horrible punishments on the Egyptian people, trying to get Pharaoh to change his mind. They suffered from locusts, famines, and plagues of all kinds. But Pharaoh's heart was made of rock. He refused to yield and kept demanding more and more work from the Israelites.

Finally God would not stand for Pharaoh's abuse any longer. God told Moses to get everyone ready to move, to be ready to go on a minute's notice. They packed their things. They grabbed food and quickly made bread. They prayed.

And then God went through Egypt, killing all the first-born males, both animals and humans, while passing over the children of Israel. Horrible cries went up as the Egyptian people realized their loss.

In despair, Pharaoh agreed that Moses could finally take his people and leave. Thousands of men, women, and children lined up and began marching toward the Red Sea. Glorious freedom awaited on the other side, but I had no idea how we would get cross the wide expanse of water. There were no boats, and it was much too far to swim. Yet Moses urged us on.

As we reached the shore, a horrible thing happened. Pharaoh changed his mind. He wanted his slaves back

and would stop at nothing to bring us all back. We could see the dust flying up across the countryside as Pharaoh's chariots thundered toward us.

Ahead of us was the Red Sea, deep and cold. Behind us were Pharaoh's fury and sharp swords. Only feet from the water's edge, babies and young mothers began to wail.

"Moses," ordered God. "Hold up your staff, and the waters will part!"

With a grand flourish, Moses lifted me to the sky. I never felt so strong! With the heavens above and the anxious people below, I watched the waters divide, just like God said they would.

Moses and I stood there all night, his arms holding me high. Our people ran across a grand path carved between two towering walls of water. As they touched land on the other side, God told Moses to put me down. Then the waters flowed over the Egyptian army, drowning them in the deluge.

God's people were finally free. No longer would they be slaves.

Today, like God's people, I also am free, yet I remain hidden away for safekeeping. Some say I will be brought out when Jesus returns. On that day, I will be honored to serve—for I will be serving the greatest shepherd of all.

QUESTIONS TO CONSIDER
YOUNGER READERS

What does it mean to be a slave? Describe what you know about slavery.

Why did God want the Israelites to be free? What might it have felt like to walk across a lake bottom with walls of water surrounding you on your way to freedom?

Do parts of this story make you happy? Do parts make you sad? Describe your feelings.

OLDER READERS

The burning bush in the wilderness is a clear symbol of Moses being called to a certain vocation, or in his case, mission. In your own wild places, what clues have you seen that might indicate a particular direction for your life?

Parting the waters of the Red Sea was a powerful act on God's part. Have you ever been in a situation where you feel that you were saved by God's grace?

The Exodus was a pivotal point in Judeo/Christian history. Jews still celebrate Passover, commemorating that holy night when God led the Israelites out of slavery into freedom. How do you reconcile biblical references to slavery (e.g. Exodus: 21:2, Ephesians 6:5) and the Epistle to Philemon, which lays out God's ardent desire for his people to be free?

THE BIBLE STORY

Exodus 14:10-16. As Pharaoh drew near, the Israelites looked back, and there were the Egyptians advancing on them. In great fear the Israelites cried out to the LORD. They said to Moses, "Was it because there are no graves in Egypt that you have taken us away to die in the wilderness? What have you done to us, bringing us out of Egypt? Is this not the very thing we told you in Egypt, 'Let us alone and let us serve the Egyptians'? For it would have been better for us to serve the Egyptians than to die in the wilderness." But Moses said to the people, "Do not be afraid, stand firm, and see the deliverance the LORD will accomplish for you today; for the Egyptians whom you see today you shall never see again. The LORD will fight for you, and you have only to keep still."

Then the LORD said to Moses, "Why do you cry out to me? Tell the Israelites to go forward. But you lift up your staff, and stretch out your hand over the sea and divide it, that the Israelites may go into the sea on dry ground."

WAITING ON GOD
As Told by the Ark of the Covenant

It is very quiet where I am. So quiet that I know each bird by its chirp or caw or tweet. So still that I can almost hear moonbeams casting their light over the cave that shelters me. So dark that when the sun's arms peek under the door each morning, they wave goodbye and move on within minutes, disappointed that I am not coming out.

I am an ark, a very special box.

"C'mon, Ark," says the sun. "Haven't you been in that cave long enough?"

"The world is a great place, Ark," say the mice who

scamper in and out of the cave. "You gotta watch out for wild cats, but there's lots to see!"

The brown bats offer, "If you want to go out at night, we'll take care of you. We'll use our supersonic powers to hear things for you. After all, arks don't usually have ears."

"Thanks friends, but I don't need help," I say. "I can hear and see just fine. My job is to hold tight and wait here. I hold the most precious items in the world—the two stone tablets on which the Ten Commandments are written. And my job is to keep them safe and stay where I am until God calls me."

Moses himself had me built out of the finest materials he could find. He had just come off Mount Sinai, his face shining like wildfire after God gave him the commandments. Here's what God had him write down:

Don't have any other gods but me.
Don't worship idols.
Don't use God's name in vain.
Respect the Sabbath, as a holy day of rest.
Honor your parents.
Don't murder.
Don't commit adultery.
Don't steal.
Don't tell lies about your neighbor.
Don't covet anything that belongs to your neighbor.

Moses had spent months with God on the mountain, and he knew the tablets had to be protected. After all, the first time Moses went up on the mountain, the people threw a big party. When Moses came back to camp, he was so angry that he broke the first set of commandments in half. That couldn't happen again.

"Build an ark!" Moses ordered. "Gather logs from the acacia trees and polish them into the finest wood, so that we may build a fitting place for the Lord's words to reside."

And I am that ark: a container built like a miniature ship, ready to travel across the land with my precious cargo. Moses had gold placed all around and inside me, so my body shone almost as much as Moses' face when he saw God. Two beautiful golden angels sat on top of me, always pointing to God. God's law would have a safe and beautiful home.

I wondered: *What will it feel like to hold the commandments? Am I worthy enough? Will my surrounding arms be sufficient to hold such a great gift?*

Moses tucked a bed of the finest white cotton from Egypt into my belly. And then he placed the heavy stone tablets down inside of me. I was surprised to feel they were

warm and somewhat soft. Stones are usually cold and hard to the touch. But these weren't. They felt *alive*.

Power and comfort passed from the tablets to me. We entered into a partnership then, one that has lasted to this day. Whenever God's people, the Israelites, traveled—through the wilderness for forty years, moving, always moving—the tablets and I went first. Moses had built rings into my sides and poles for carrying, so God's Law would always lead the way.

God had a special place in mind for the people, a forever home, and my job was to help them get there.

Keep the rules, I reminded the people silently. *Obey the commandments, and you will make it all the way home.*

This is a covenant—an agreement. You keep your part, and I will do my part. This covenant was God's promise to the people that they would reach the Promised Land.

One day Moses dragged himself into my tent. His face looked like spider webs were etched across it, but there were no spiders, just too much worry.

He prayed, "Help me, Lord! What does your holy law say about unruly people? They are tired, and they complain all the time. How do I keep their spirits up?" Moses asked. "They are hungry. They miss the sweet melons, fresh cucumbers, and tangy onions we had back in Egypt."

"Hmmm," said God. "I am not your chef, but I will see what I can do."

The next morning flakes of soft, beautiful bread called manna floated down to the Israelite camps, courtesy of God's heavenly kitchens. Skinny, hungry children raced to pick up the fluffy food.

"My people will never go hungry again," said God. "Keep reminding them that they are my people and I shall be their God!"

Yet Moses still didn't seem as joyful as God wanted.

"What's wrong?"

Moses shook his head wearily. "I am exhausted. Moving all these people across the wilderness is not an easy job."

"Find seventy men to help you, Moses," God said. "Surely you have seventy good men among all the tribes."

So Moses looked, and he found seventy good helpers. Life was easier for him then, although he still worked harder than anyone I have ever seen.

On those long wilderness marches, power flowed from Moses, from me, from all of us. If you asked me to describe it, I couldn't. Does a light bulb know its source? Does it need to? My job was simply to be what God had made me to be: a presence of the Lord amongst the people. We each have a power within us that flows out to make a difference in this world. Mine is to house and honor the commandments.

Moses died before we entered the Promised Land. But the Lord kept his promise. A new leader named Joshua took Moses' place, and God continued using me in special ways to help lead the Israelites into the land of promise.

"We must cross over the Jordan River," Joshua told the people, "to enter the land God has promised us."

"But it's a very great river, full and flowing!" his helpers said. "There are a lot of us, and some of us can't swim! How will we get everyone across?"

Others cried: "This is not what we bargained for. We know all about deserts and mountains and sand, but this much water, never mind all those big, tough people who live on the other side…"

The people had great fear. God spoke to Joshua and told him to use me to part the waters of the great river so the people could cross into the Promised Land.

"Are you sure about this?" asked the generals.

"Absolutely!" said Joshua, trusting in the power God put into me. On the appointed day, twelve of Israel's priests carried me down to the river.

"Step into the water," Joshua told them. When the first priest put his foot into the water, the waters rolled back, all the way back up the river to the next town! As long as the priests held me up in the middle of the riverbed, the land was dry. And everyone— hundreds of thousands of people—crossed over into the Promised Land.

"We are here!" Joshua shouted.

"Wow," people exclaimed. "We made it, just like God promised!"

But the job wasn't done yet. A huge city called Jericho loomed over us, a fortress with sky-high walls. The townspeople were fierce warriors, so we had no choice but to fight.

"The Lord will lead our way," Joshua told the people. "Take the ark, carry it in front of our armies, and blow the trumpets. We will march around the city."

We marched around that city for six days, with me leading the way. And on the seventh day, with a "*Tra-taaa*" from a ram's horn, the walls of that great city fell down. We were finally free to live in the land God promised us.

God's people began to settle into the new territory. They built houses, towns, and palaces. They began to feel comfortable, and some of the toughness the people developed in their wilderness marches began to disappear.

One day King David, a tall handsome man with curly dark hair, called in his chief advisor, the prophet Nathan. It was evening, and David was walking in the garden where I was resting in the holy tent. Like Moses before him, David would often come to spend time with me and to pray about what the Lord wanted.

"Nathan," David said, "I live in this really nice palace. I have nice chairs and tables and gold on the walls. I have servants and people to play music and cook good food. The walls are high and beautiful. I am a powerful ruler."

Blushing a little, David added, "You know, people all over look to me and call upon me as the Lord's favorite one."

"Yes, I have heard those rumors," said Nathan.

"Well, I have been wondering," David said. "Maybe I should give the ark a more permanent home. A real house for it to live in. Then we would always know where the Lord...I mean the ark...is, safe and secure!"

A chill passed through me. *What? Lock me up? Lock up God?*

How could you lock up God? God is free to be within the rushing winds or the beautiful sunrise. God is free to enter into the home of a sick child or stand by the side of a newborn baby, to stride down battlefields and enter into the deepest reaches of outer space.

Nathan went home that night and prayed to the Lord. The next day, he returned to David and told him what the Lord had said.

"God came to me in a dream, and God told me to say to you: 'And who, David are you, to put me in a box!? You have let your power go to your head. Yes, I have favored you—and yes, you have become a man among men. But I am the Lord. And I am not to be bound.'"

David listened to Nathan, his trusted adviser, and did not build the house or lock up the ark. But his son Solomon did.

Solomon, whom some called "Solomon the Wise," eventually thought that he was wiser than everyone else. His temple in Jerusalem was looked upon as if it were the only House of God—instead of the whole world being God's house and the ark just a small piece of God's power and presence in this world.

Solomon and his people locked me away deep inside the temple, boxed within a box, where hardly anyone would come to visit me or seek the Lord's voice from within me.

Over time different powers and kingdoms rose and fell and rose, until a powerful army from Babylon came and destroyed Jerusalem and the temple. It was a terrible time.

The invaders took the people and almost all of the objects from the temple into exile, to places far away from their homes.

But I said *almost all...*

Jeremiah was one of God's great prophets, a living, human voice of God. Jeremiah understood what was happening, so before the Babylonian invaders arrived, he took me from the temple. He put me into a cave on Moses' mountain and sealed up the entrance to keep me safe.

He said, "This place shall remain hidden until God gathers the people together again and shows mercy."

Where we are is a holy secret. What's important is that the tablets and I are safe. And that I am waiting—waiting and ready for God to call me out again.

QUESTIONS TO CONSIDER
YOUNGER READERS

Why do parents make rules for families? Why did God give the Ten Commandments to Moses?

If you were to write rules for all the people in the world, what would they be?

God wants us to have the commandments written in our hearts, and people have memorized them for thousands of years. See if you can memorize them and say them out loud to a parent or grandparent.

OLDER READERS

The ark was a moveable sign of God's presence and belonged to no individual, but to all God's people. What symbols of God's presence do you treasure and why?

The Ark of the Covenant has a unique place in religious history. Some say it currently resides in Ethiopia, under heavy guard. Others say it resides under the ruins of the first temple in Jerusalem that was destroyed by the Babylonians in 586 BC, now site of the Dome of the Rock. This account of the ark's location is taken from 2 Maccabees 2. What have you read and seen about the ark and its significance, location, and history?

What are your beliefs about the ark? Have your beliefs changed after reading this story? If so, how?

THE BIBLE STORY

2 Maccabees 2:1-8. "One finds in the records that the prophet Jeremiah ordered those who were being deported to take some of the fire, as has been mentioned, and that the prophet, after giving them the law, instructed those who were being deported not to forget the commandments of the LORD, or to be led astray in their thoughts on seeing the gold and silver statues and their adornment. And with other similar words he exhorted them that the law should not depart from their hearts.

It was also in the same document that the prophet, having received an oracle, ordered that the tent and the ark should follow with him, and that he went out to the mountain where Moses had gone up and had seen the inheritance of God. Jeremiah came and found a cave-dwelling, and he brought there the tent and the ark and the altar of incense; then he sealed up the entrance. Some of those who followed him came up intending to mark the way, but could not find it. When Jeremiah learned of it, he rebuked them and declared: "The place shall remain unknown until God gathers his people together again and shows his mercy. Then the LORD will disclose these things, and the glory of the LORD and the cloud will appear, as they were shown in the case of Moses, and as Solomon asked that the place should be specially consecrated."

STOP HITTING ME!
As Told by the Talking Donkey

It was dark. Completely dark, except for the stars. And I was doing what I liked most: grazing under those stars, alone, soaking in the night air and feeling free. No one bothers me at night. All day long I work, pulling unbearably heavy loads. I don't prance around like a fancy horse—I work! Nighttime is my time.

And alone in that darkness was when I saw it—a huge pillar of fire, dancing in the river valley below me. Sizzling, burning, and twisting, the fire reached from sky to ground, lighting dark gorges and hollowed-out canyons for miles. Red and orange and yellow hues tumbled together as one, changing with every second.

Transfixed, I stared for hours. I wanted to run behind it, to see where it would go, to revel in its power. As the sun rose, I could see thousands of people doing just that—marching and dancing behind the amazing pillar of fire.

We were used to strangers in Moab, my country. We often fought them, for we believed they would take our land. But we had never seen anything like this pillar of fire before—or so many people in one place. We wouldn't stand a chance in a fight against them.

I guess I wasn't the only one who was worried because later that day, two huffy-looking men came looking for my owner, Balaam. He's a diviner. People believe that if he curses people, bad things will happen to them—and if he blesses them, good things will happen. Balaam gets a lot of business.

The guys were rich, I could tell. Fancy robes, lots of jewelry, snooty horses trying to get at my grass. Once the men were inside, I edged up to an open window to hear their conversation.

"Balaam," one of the men said, "Our king, Balak, needs you to curse all of these strangers coming through Moab. You're just the one to squash them like vermin into the ground. Wave your hands and say a curse, and we'll be done with the lot of them!"

As far as I could see, the people following the pillar of fire weren't causing any trouble. It seemed like they were just passing through. But then I'm just a donkey, not a know-it-all horse.

"Stay here tonight," Balaam told the two men. "I'll see what God says, and let you know my answer in the morning."

I could see the men roll their eyes. Later, when they went outside, I heard one say: "Yeah, right. This old man is gonna talk to God. And then he'll tell us what God says to him?!! First of all, there is no God—only magic. And even if there was a God, who does this guy think he is that God would come and talk to him?"

There was so much these men did not know. But being as snooty as their horses, the men tried to tempt Balaam with a big bag of money. "Take this gold, Balaam! And there's more where this came from. Just curse these people for us and be done with it!"

The answer from Balaam was not the one they wanted.

"Go away," said Balaam. "God warned me not to interfere with the strangers crossing our land. I will not curse them. And I advise you not to lay a hand on them either!"

Shaking their fists, the men rode away. Two days later, other officials came, loaded down with even more money, once again begging Balaam to curse the strangers.

"The king needs you to curse these people!" cried the men. "Just wave your arms around and curse them and they will die. Our problem will be solved! It's easy—and we'll give you anything you want in return!"

"I don't do anything unless I check with God first," said Balaam. "Stay here tonight. I'll see what God wants me to do."

God came to Balaam that night and said, "Since these men have come all this way to see you, go ahead and ride with them to where the strangers are marching and dancing. But don't do anything else unless I say so."

The men were thrilled—Balaam less so. Still, Balaam saddled me up the next morning, and we started off, with the king's men in front. As we rode, I could hear Balaam talking to himself, almost chanting.

"Listen for God's voice," he half-sang to himself. "Listen for God's voice…Listen…"

Suddenly, ten feet in front of my nose stood a huge angel, right in the middle of the road. The angel was at least twelve feet tall, the size of a tree, and brandished a golden sword. With wings outstretched, the magnificent creature whipped the giant sword back and forth, back and forth.

Well, I wasn't going to get near that thing or that sword! It could slice me—and Balaam—into pieces! So I did what any self-respecting donkey would do—I swerved down into the ditch to avoid the angel.

"What are you doing?" yelled Balaam, hitting me with the reins. "Get back on the road!"

It was then I realized that Balaam couldn't see the angel! When I looked back up, the angel had disappeared.

But two hours later, it showed up again—this time in the middle of a vineyard.

Have you ever been in a vineyard? There's not much room, with grape vines standing in tight rows like school desks. We were standing right next to a stone wall, and when I veered into the wall to avoid the angel, I accidentally crushed Balaam's foot. Once more, he beat me.

"What is the matter with you?" he yelled. "I've never seen you like this!"

What is the matter with you? I thought. *Stop hitting me!*

Wearily, I limped along. All that hitting was really painful. And then, as we were going through another tight alley, the angel appeared again, right in front of me. I couldn't go forward. I couldn't go backward. Doing the only thing I could think of, I sat down. And oops—Balaam fell off my back. He was really, really, really mad. He started attacking me with a sharp stick, thrashing my sides and back.

"Ouch! Stop! Don't hit me!"

In that terrible moment, God gave me the gift of speech.

"What have I ever done to you that you have beat me these three times?!!" I cried out.

Balaam's eyes opened wide—his donkey was talking?! In disbelief, he stammered: "B-b-b-b-because you've been playing games with me! If I had a sword, I would have killed you by now!"

"Am I not your trusted donkey on whom you've ridden for years? Have I ever done anything like this to you before? Have I?"

"No," said Balaam.

And then God opened Balaam's eyes. The old man saw the angel standing right there in our path, twisting his sword like figure eights. Hands over his head, Balaam fell to the ground, his face in the dirt.

"Why have you beaten your poor donkey these three times?" asked the angel. "I came here to block your way because you're getting yourself into deep and dangerous trouble. The donkey saw me and turned away from me these three times. If she hadn't, I would have killed you by now—but not the donkey. I would have let her live."

"I have sinned," Balaam said. "I had no idea you were standing in the road blocking my way. Perhaps I should go home."

"No, follow the king's men. But only say what I tell you to say—no other word."

Whew. I could barely breathe. Not only had I seen an angel of the Lord, but God had stuck up for me—had given me a voice.

Balaam and I trailed the king's men for several weeks. At every turn, they tried to encourage him to curse the outsiders.

As we listened and watched, Balaam realized that God loved the people traveling through our land. They were the children of Israel, journeying to reach the place God wanted them to be—the Promised Land, the land of milk and honey. Like us, they were listening for God's voice with every step.

Ah, journeys in the wilderness. Turns out that the beautiful pillar of fire I had spotted earlier was the Lord's way of guiding the strangers through our land. God wanted them to know where they were going—and to provide comfort so they would not be scared. God was protecting them, leading them, giving them strength and courage. It was just like the way God protected me, sending an angel to stand in my path and giving me the gift of speech so I could stick up for myself!

And isn't that God's way? To provide us with help and remind us to always listen for God's voice.

QUESTIONS TO CONSIDER
YOUNGER READERS

Wow! A talking donkey! How cool is that? What's your reaction?

God stepped in and gave the donkey a voice because her owner was beating her, and that was wrong. Have you spoken up when someone hurt you? What did you say? Why is it important to tell someone you trust if you are being hurt?

Sometimes we get hurt and we feel we might get in more trouble if we say something, yet God always hears our pain. Was there ever a time when you were hurt but felt like you couldn't say anything? If that happens again, know you are not alone, for God is always with you, every second of every day.

OLDER READERS

Aside from the serpent talking to Eve in Genesis, this is the only story of an animal speaking in the Bible. Why did God choose this particular moment to respond in such a powerful and unusual way?

Profound theological implications run through this story: God not only stands up for the voiceless and oppressed—even those in the animal kingdom—but God also gives the donkey a voice so that she may rise up to protect herself. What might this mean for God's entire kingdom? What might this mean for those who suffer at the hands of others?

God put an angel in the donkey's path. The word angel means "messenger of God." In times of crisis in your life, have you ever experienced angels directing you, comforting you, leading you? What was their appearance? Is it possible that modern-day angels might look different from ancient ones?

THE BIBLE STORY

Numbers 22:20-35. That night God came to Balaam and said to him, "If the men have come to summon you, get up and go with them; but do only what I tell you to do." So Balaam got up in the morning, saddled his donkey, and went with the officials of Moab.

God's anger was kindled because he was going, and the angel of the LORD took his stand in the road as his adversary. Now he was riding on the donkey, and his two servants were with him. The donkey saw the angel of the LORD standing in the road, with a drawn sword in his hand; so the donkey turned off the road, and went into the field; and Balaam struck the donkey, to turn it back on to the road. Then the angel of the LORD stood in a narrow path between the vineyards, with a wall on either side. When the donkey saw the angel of the LORD, it scraped against the wall, and scraped Balaam's foot against the wall; so he struck it again. Then the angel of the LORD went ahead, and stood in a narrow place, where there was no way to turn either to the right or to the left. When the donkey saw the angel of the LORD, it lay down under Balaam; and Balaam's anger was kindled, and he struck the donkey with his staff. Then the LORD opened the mouth of the donkey, and it said to Balaam, "What have I done to you, that you have struck me these three times?" Balaam said to the donkey, "Because you have made a fool of me! I wish I had a sword in my hand! I would kill you right now!" But the donkey said to Balaam, "Am I not your donkey, which you have ridden all your life to this day? Have I been in the habit of treating you this way?" And he said, "No."

Then the LORD opened the eyes of Balaam, and he saw the angel of the LORD standing in the road, with his drawn sword in his hand; and he bowed down, falling on his face. The angel of the LORD said to him, "Why have you struck your donkey these three times? I have come out as an adversary, because your way is perverse before me. The donkey saw me, and turned away from me these three times. If it had not turned away from me, surely just now I would have killed you and let it live." Then Balaam said to the angel of the LORD, "I have sinned, for I did not know that you were standing in the road to oppose me. Now therefore, if it is displeasing to you, I will return home." The angel of the LORD said to Balaam, "Go with the men; but speak only what I tell you to speak." So Balaam went on with the officials of Balak.

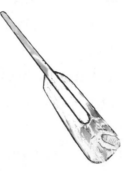

JESUS: MASTER OF WIND, WAVES, AND FEAR

As Told by Gordy the Fishing Boat

There I was on the beach, stretched out like a tomcat with a full meal in his belly. Good thing, too, for dark and angry storm clouds had been moving in all day. It didn't matter now, though—I was in for the night. No moon. No stars. Just surging chaos out on the waves.

In case you hadn't guessed, I'm a fishing boat on the Sea of Galilee. Nothing fancy. My friends call me Gordy. I'm what you might call a "renter." Different fishermen take me out onto the water. I got stranded on the beach about a year ago after my owner, Simon, left for a different line of work. I don't know if I will see him again. I miss him terribly, but there's not much I can do about it. He was hot on the trail of a man called Jesus.

The day Simon left was the craziest thing I ever saw. We had just come in to shore after fishing all night. We hadn't caught a dang thing, and we were tired, dirty, and grouchy. Simon was washing himself off in the water, like fishermen do. Next thing I knew, a guy named Jesus came along and asked Simon and me to take him out in the water about twenty feet. Turned out he had dozens of people on his heels, crowding him. But Jesus didn't want to get away from them. He just wanted a place where they could see him and hear him talk about God.

I thought Simon would ignore him. That's what I was doing. After all, we were both ready to sleep. Besides, talking about God? Um, this was a beach, not a synagogue!

But Simon had a heart. A huge heart. That was part of why I always loved him. More than once, I had seen him jump in the water to save people who thought they could swim but couldn't. And almost every day, I witnessed him pulling baby fish out of our nets so they could swim away and grow up.

Next thing I knew, I was back in the water. What was going on? Kids ran along the beach. Some people sat with their feet in the water. Others stood, nodding their heads and occasionally laughing. They weren't laughing at Jesus but with him. There was something about Jesus that just made everyone feel happy. The crowd grew. And grew.

Soon about a hundred people crowded the beach to listen to Jesus. He talked about God and about love. About how he was there in the beginning when the world was made. About how God knows us down to our very bones—or sterns and bows, as the case may be.

I could tell Simon was listening. He was sitting where he always does, in the back of the boat, with his hand on the rudder.

I guess Jesus saw something special in Simon. When we were back on shore, Jesus pulled Simon aside.

"Come with me," Jesus said. "I could use your help. You catch fish right now. But I will show you how to catch people!"

And that was it. My strong, rugged friend with whom I had weathered so many storms suddenly had a new job.

Simon washed me out, caulked over a couple of thin places, and then dragged me over to his fishermen friends. Eyes red but voice strong, he said simply, "Take care of Gordy. He's a good boat."

And then Simon was gone. I heard from another boat family down the shore, the Zebedees, that their sons James and John had gone with Jesus too.

🔑 🔑 🔑

I stayed on my own for about a year and was rented out to other fishermen on most days. Life wasn't so bad. I could have been left to rot. Or torn into firewood. Or crashed up along the rocks. At least I was safe in the waters I knew so well.

But one night, the mist blowing off the waves wrapped around me like a cold, dead fish. And talk about lack of visibility—I couldn't see a thing on land or sea. It was not a fit night for man nor boat.

But apparently some people decided to brave the storm. I heard muffled voices come toward me on the beach.

Who would be out on a night like this? I wondered.

"We need to cross over to the other side," said one man.

"Are you kidding?" exclaimed another. "It's dark out there. And stormy. It's too dangerous to be out."

"Let's wait until morning!" said a third.

Good idea, I thought. *You should definitely wait until morning. It is dangerous out there.*

But the man who had spoken first was insistent.

"It's time," he said, with a voice that sounded like he expected his suggestion to be followed. "Find a boat. We're going."

I snugged down in the sand, secure in the knowledge that even if they went out, I would be safe. They wouldn't want me. They would take one of the newer, sleeker boats. I'm not exactly what you call waterproof, even on good days.

Human feet lingered around my shinier boat friends.

"Not those," said one of the men. "Not any of those."

Hmm...Something about that voice sounded familiar.

"Nope, not that one," the voice said, getting closer.

And then, the feet stopped in front of me, slightly apart, the way fishermen stand.

Something about those sandals looked familiar.

"Gordy, is that you? Remember me?"

No. It couldn't be. Simon? Simon?!

"I've missed you, buddy. And I really need your help."

It was Simon! He had lost some weight and wasn't quite as brawny as I remembered, but he was the same man I had come to know so well, with the same strong arms that had hauled me in and out of the water for years.

If I could have jumped up and thrown my sails around this man, I would have.

"I have our boat!" Simon yelled. "This one will keep us safe!"

At that moment I could have cared less about the storm blowing in. All I wanted was to be with my old friend. Thirteen men squeezed on board, including the man called Jesus, and off we went toward the other side of the lake. It was really crazy, I know. But when someone you love calls you to do something, to be part of something, you say, "Yes." You might not get the chance again.

But it wasn't long before I started regretting my decision. Water soon poured over my sides, and the waves were like headstrong camels tossing us up and down. Several of the men threw up over my sides, and my sails were soon pulled down. The men rowed as if their lives depended on it. Because they did.

The only one who seemed to not be paying any attention was Jesus. There he was, asleep in the back of the boat like he didn't have a care in the world.

"Wake him up!" shouted one of the men.

Another cried: "Jesus, don't you care if we live or die?"

Jesus' eyelids fluttered open, and slowly he came to his feet. Standing—and I don't know how he kept his balance—he reached out his hand toward the sea.

"Quiet!" he said. "Settle down!" At once, the wind and water obeyed. The lake stilled, the water became like glass, and the wind dropped to a whisper. Stars emerged from their hiding places, and a crescent moon appeared. I could have sworn the moonlight reached down and surrounded Jesus like a hug.

"Don't be such cowards," said Jesus, looking at the men. "Don't you have any faith at all? Have courage, my friends!"

Wow. In all my years on this great big lake I had experienced a lot of storms, but I had never seen anyone control the weather.

We sailed to the other side of the lake after that, arriving just as the sun rose. By the time we landed, I learned Simon had been given a new name by Jesus. He was called Peter—it means "Rock"—and he was Jesus' first mate.

I also discovered something important about Jesus. The master of wind and waves and fear, Jesus was God's man for sure.

I have been doing my part ever since that night, carrying Peter and Jesus and the other disciples all over the lakes of Galilee. We don't look for fish anymore. We look for people—people who are scared and sick or those who make room for Jesus in their hearts. It's the best job I've ever had.

🚶 🚶 🚶

QUESTIONS TO CONSIDER
YOUNGER READERS

Why do you think Jesus was sleeping when everyone else thought they might drown? What enabled him to be so relaxed?

What do you think it felt like to see Jesus calm the waves and winds so quickly? How would you have felt if your boat almost capsized and then, in an instant, Jesus made everything calm?

Have you ever been in a boat or plane or train and felt scared? Ask your parents how they call on God when they feel scared.

OLDER READERS

Simon left his job for Jesus. How would you have responded? What is your reaction when faced with a risky proposal?

Name a time when you've felt scared. How did you find God in the midst of fear and chaos?

The wind and the waves obeyed Jesus instantly. They seemed to know him well. Do you think they had talked before? Do you think they knew Jesus from the moment of creation? What does this story say about forces of nature and their relationship with the Creator?

Many of the stories of our faith take place around water: the Israelites crossing the Red Sea; John the Baptist baptizing Jesus in the River Jordan; Jesus finding his first disciples by the Sea of Galilee; the Samaritan woman by the well who was quizzing Jesus; Peter trying to walk on water and being rescued by Jesus; Lydia listening to Paul at a river near Philippi; Jesus being pierced by a sword on the cross and having water gush from his side, which we remember in the eucharist. What does water mean in your faith life? Are there ways in which the Holy Spirit is working through water in your life?

THE BIBLE STORY

Mark 4:35-41. On that day, when evening had come, he said to them, "Let us go across to the other side." And leaving the crowd behind, they took him with them in the boat, just as he was. Other boats were with him. A great windstorm arose, and the waves beat into the boat, so that the boat was already being swamped. But he was in the stern, asleep on the cushion; and they woke him up and said to him, "Teacher, do you not care that we are perishing?" He woke up and rebuked the wind, and said to the sea, "Peace! Be still!" Then the wind ceased, and there was dead calm. He said to them, "Why are you afraid? Have you still no faith?" And they were filled with great awe and said to one another, "Who then is this, that even the wind and the sea obey him?"

THE WOMAN AT THE WELL: SPARRING WITH JESUS
As Told by the Water Jug

I can't move. I can't wave. I can't even tip myself over. But I carry something so important that no one can live without it. Can you guess what I am?

I'm a water jug—one of hundreds in my little town! When I was working about 2,000 years ago, there was no running water, no electricity. Most everyone went to the town well each morning to get water. Everyone, that is, but me.

Each morning I saw my friends being picked up by their ceramic ears and swung around by laughing girls. They were happy to be out in the cool morning air with their friends.

"C'mon!" the girls would say, gliding down the hard-packed dirt trail, with my fellow jugs balanced on their heads. "I can beat you, even when this thing is full of water! Did you see those cute shepherds who came into town last night? There were five, maybe six…"

I didn't get to go with them, because my owner wasn't one of those young, happy, laughing girls. She was a widow who had been married five times. People teased her and made fun of her.

Instead of going to the well in the morning with the others, I stayed by the side of the house until there was no more shade. When the sun hit the high point in the sky, when everyone else in town was hot and tired and ready for an afternoon nap, my owner would pick me up and head to the well for water. She figured that no one would be around then to give her a hard time.

If jugs could droop, I would have. My life was so dang lonely. It was almost as lonely as my owner's.

That was the way it was back then. If your husband died, you married his brother. If he died, you married the next brother. Women didn't have the freedom to hold regular jobs. If you were a widow, you normally ended up on the street, homeless and hungry unless you could find someone to marry. It was a hard life. As a result of her troubles, my owner tended to be a bit sarcastic, acting tough, as if nothing—or no one—could hurt her anymore.

♟ ♟ ♟

When we approached the well that day, I felt her shoulders arch, tipping me a bit to the right, then to the left. Her breathing got faster. Her teeth clamped down. Then I saw why: A man was by the well, a single man sitting against a tree. His head hung between drawn-up knees. As we approached, he stood up, then sat back down. Sweat dripped from his brow. He seemed a bit shaky.

One word went through my jarhead: Tired. The guy looked exhausted.

"Please, give me a drink of water," he said.

"How is it, that you, a Jew, talks to me, a woman of Samaria?" my mistress asked.

Just give him the water! I thought. *The guy's obviously exhausted, give him a drink.* But no. Like a cat with a mouse, she was going to tease him first.

In those days, men didn't usually talk to women they didn't know. And Jews and Samaritans? Well, they were cousins of a sort but also age-old enemies. Hundreds of years before, Jews and Samaritans had all been in the same tribe, but unfortunately their ancestors had quarreled. Now Samaritans didn't even like to see Jews walk through our lands. Sadly, the Jews felt the same way about the Samaritans. No talking or trespassing allowed!

But this man was different. He didn't seem defensive, murderous, territorial, or even angry.

"If you knew the gift of God," he said, "and who it is that is saying to you, 'Give me a drink,' you would have asked him and he would have given you living water."

"Sir, you don't even have a bucket!" scoffed my owner.

Ah, we're in for it now, I thought. Sometimes in her bristly defensiveness, my owner talked to people like she was flipping fish in a frying pan: hot, quick, and sizzling. She could sauté people even before they even knew they were on the grill.

"Anyone who drinks the living water will never thirst," he replied.

"Sure," she said, drawing out the word. "Give me that water, so I'll never have to come back here again!"

And then a zinger came from the man: "Go get your husband and bring him back here."

Ouch.

My owner replied: "I have no husband."

"That's right!" said the man. "You do not have a husband—you've had five, and the man you're living with now isn't your husband!"

Boom! How did he know that?

"Oh, so you're a prophet, are you?" my owner asked defensively.

Prophets are a big deal. Like my owner, they can be a bit ornery. And they are always telling people to do this and don't do that, to shape up. They represent God, and we try to listen but their warnings can be grim.

And we'd had a bunch of prophets: Isaiah, Jeremiah, Amos, and many more. But we had not seen the prophet called the Messiah. Samaritans and Jews alike believed that the Messiah, God's strong and blazing son, would one day stand upon the earth and save us all from evil.

"When the Messiah comes, he will straighten all this out," my mistress said.

"You don't have to look for him to come. He's here," the man said. "Right in front of you."

For once, my owner was speechless. Eyebrows shooting up, her mouth and eyes flew open.

"No," she stammered. "You...you...you...can't be!"

He looked at her with love and knowledge and joy that seemed to go straight to her heart. And I swear he looked at me the same way: a deep gaze that seemed to take in everything about me.

In that moment, there was silence. Then my owner threw me down by the side of the well and raced back to the town. I could hear her calling out as she ran: "I've just met a man who knows everything I've ever done! Do you think this could be the Messiah? Come and see for yourselves!"

And they did. As soon as the news broke, townspeople came to question the man, to look at him, to wonder, and to believe.

After my owner ran to town, I was alone with the Messiah, and in those few precious moments, a deep sense of peace came over me. I felt filled to the brim with joy.

Then the Messiah picked me up, dipped me down into the well, and put me to his mouth to draw a long cool, drink of water. Then we sat together in the shade.

In that moment, I had never felt more water filled, more living water filled, in my whole jugly life!

QUESTIONS TO CONSIDER
YOUNGER READERS

When you talk with God, what feelings do you share? The woman at the well was tired and cranky when she first started talking with Jesus—and happy by the end of the conversation. This story reminds us that God wants to hear from us no matter what we are feeling.

Jesus wanted to hear everything this woman had to say. Picture yourself sitting beside Jesus. What would you tell him?

Prayer is simply talking with God and Jesus. Do you try to talk with God every day? Why do you think that might be a good idea?

OLDER READERS

The conversation between Jesus and the woman by the well in John 4 is the longest recorded conversation that Jesus has with anyone in scripture. What does that say about her? About Jesus? About us?

Jesus met this woman exactly where she was: physically, spiritually, and emotionally. Do you ever believe you have to change before you can encounter Jesus? What does this story tell you about this belief?

Hidden not too far below the surface in this conversation is humor. How do you find humor in your spiritual life? How can it be a valuable asset?

THE BIBLE STORY

John 4:1-42. Now when Jesus learned that the Pharisees had heard, "Jesus is making and baptizing more disciples than John"—although it was not Jesus himself but his disciples who baptized—he left Judea and started back to Galilee.

But he had to go through Samaria. So he came to a Samaritan city called Sychar, near the plot of ground that Jacob had given to his son Joseph. Jacob's well was there, and Jesus, tired out by his journey, was sitting by the well. It was about noon. A Samaritan woman came to draw water, and Jesus said to her, "Give me a drink." (His disciples had gone to the city to buy food.) The Samaritan woman said to him, "How is it that you, a Jew, ask a drink of me, a woman of Samaria?" (Jews do not share things in common with Samaritans.) Jesus answered her, "If you knew the gift of God, and who it is that is saying to you, 'Give me a drink,' you would have asked him, and he would have given you living water." The woman said to him, "Sir, you have no bucket, and the well is deep. Where do you get that living water? Are you greater than our ancestor Jacob, who gave us the well, and with his sons and his flocks drank from it?" Jesus said to her, "Everyone who drinks of this water will be thirsty again, but those who drink of the water that I will give them will never be thirsty. The water that I will give will become in them a spring of water gushing up to eternal life." The woman said to him, "Sir, give me this water, so that I may never be thirsty or have to keep coming here to draw water." Jesus said to her, "Go, call your husband, and come back." The woman answered him, "I have no husband." Jesus said to her, "You are right in saying, 'I have no husband'; for you have had five husbands, and the one you have now is not your husband. What you have said is true!" The woman said to him, "Sir, I see that you are a prophet. Our ancestors worshiped on this mountain, but you say that the place where people must worship is in Jerusalem." Jesus said to her, "Woman, believe me, the hour is coming when you will worship the Father neither on this mountain nor in Jerusalem. You worship what you do not know; we worship what we know, for salvation is from the Jews. But the hour is coming, and is now here, when the true worshipers will worship the Father in spirit and truth, for the Father seeks such as these to worship him. God is spirit, and those who worship him must worship in spirit and truth." The woman said to him, "I know that Messiah is coming" (who is called Christ). "When he comes, he will proclaim all things to us." Jesus said to her, "I am he, the one who is speaking to you."

Just then his disciples came. They were astonished that he was speaking with a woman, but no one said, "What do you want?" or, "Why are you speaking with her?" Then the woman left her water jar and went back to the city. She said to the people, "Come and see a man who told me everything I have ever done! He cannot be the Messiah, can he?" They left the city and were on their way to him. Meanwhile the disciples were urging him, "Rabbi, eat something." But he said to them, "I have food to eat that you do not know about." So the disciples said to one another, "Surely no one has brought him something to eat?" Jesus said to them, "My food is to do the will of him who sent me and to complete his work. Do you not say, 'Four months more, then comes the harvest'? But I tell you, look around you, and see how the fields are ripe for harvesting. The reaper is already receiving wages and is gathering fruit for eternal life, so that sower and reaper may rejoice together. For here the saying holds true, 'One sows and another reaps.' I sent you to reap that for which you did not labor. Others have labored, and you have entered into their labor." Many Samaritans from that city believed in him because of the woman's testimony, "He told me everything I have ever done." So when the Samaritans came to him, they asked him to stay with them; and he stayed there two days. And many more believed because of his word. They said to the woman, "It is no longer because of what you said that we believe, for we have heard for ourselves, and we know that this is truly the Savior of the world."

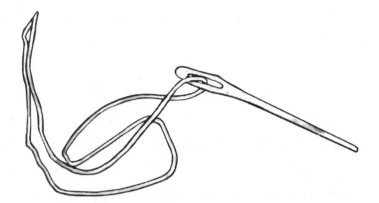

DORCAS: HER FINEST HOUR
As Told by the Sewing Needle

I am a sewing needle, made from the whitened antlers of a gazelle. Faster than almost any other animal, gazelles are always on the go, bounding and sprinting all day long.

That describtion also perfectly fit Dorcas, whose name meant "gazelle" in Greek. Fired up by God's love, her ministry was simple: She created warm and beautiful coats for the poor widows of Joppa, a seaside town thirty-five miles north of Jerusalem.

You can think of me as the "assistant gazelle," racing up and down each day through mountains of fabric. In and out, up and down. Tireless. Strong. And when Dorcas wasn't sewing, I would ride on her wrist, tucked into a puffy pin cushion she wore like other women wear shiny bracelets.

I loved our travel days. With her arms full of warm cloaks, Dorcas would walk the cold streets and back alleys of Joppa, handing out her creations to women in need. She knew where to find those folks: behind buildings, on benches, and especially down by the seashore. Seeing those women so cold and lonely broke my needle heart.

These women would stand on the water's edge, shivering, eyes scanning the horizon, hoping for their sailor husbands to return. When husbands died, poverty and hunger came quickly. Being a widow was tough because women were not allowed to hold paying jobs back then.

I heard Dorcas talking with a trembling woman and her three young children.

"We come here every day," the woman whispered. "His boat washed up empty two weeks ago. But I know he'll come back."

"We never had much money but there was always food on the table," said the woman. "But now we're so hungry, and it's getting colder every night. My oldest boy fishes for us, but he hasn't caught anything in three days."

Tears burst forth. "I'm so scared we won't make it through the winter!"

Dorcas held out a bundle of coats. "Find something that will keep you warm. And bring your children to my house today! I live right across from the market—in the two-story blue house. I have warm coats for the children as well and as much food as you all can eat."

"You are sent from God!" cried the woman. She reached into the pile and pulled out a full-length woolen cloak with a hood and matching gloves embroidered in scarlet and ivory. Not only would the woman stay warm, but she would also feel and look beautiful!

Dorcas and I continued our trek down the shore, handing out coats until we had given them all away.

Later that morning, the woman from the shore and her children knocked on Dorcas's door. Their eyes grew wide when they saw the activity inside. About a dozen neighborhood women were sewing, praying, singing, preparing lunch, and laughing.

"Come in, come in!" said the women. "We've been praying you would stop by!"

Dorcas's house was simply a fun place. Some of her friends had been homeless themselves. Others were widows, and their days had been empty and joyless until they came to the house with Dorcas. Still others had seen their children grow up and move away. Everyone found both friends and work at Dorcas's home.

Those who had food brought what they had and shared it. Those who could sew came early and stayed late. Women with extra money donated wool, yarn, and thread.

Like the stitches, prayers wove through the coats, in and out, in and out.

"Lord, we don't know who will wear this coat," prayed an old woman as she attached long sleeves to a thick gray coat. "But we pray that it will keep her warm and bring her comfort."

"May it be so," said the group. "Amen!"

Talk of Jesus ran through the conversations like music, for one of the women had seen him transform five loaves of bread and two fish into food for five thousand! Another had seen Jesus heal her son of his blindness. Talk of Jesus was talk of hope.

And then, just as lunch was being served, the door flew open. In rushed Priscilla, a young woman who was almost as busy as Dorcas: sewing, singing, helping to deliver coats, fixing the next meal, and keeping the oil lamps full.

"You'll never believe who I saw!" she said, her cheeks flushed with excitement.

"Who?"

"Peter, Jesus' disciple! Peter is at Lydda!"

Priscilla was so excited that she could barely get the words out. Peter was a big deal, and Lydda was only a day's walk away! One of Jesus' closest friends, Peter had been at Jesus' side for all the travels, the miracles, and the stories. He had even walked on water—until he got scared and started to drown and Jesus had to rescue him. And Peter was the one Jesus had named as the rock of his newborn church!

"Peter was telling everybody what it was like to be on the road with Jesus!" exclaimed Priscilla. "He told us about how Jesus touched crippled people and they got up and danced and how Jesus died and was in the tomb for three days and then showed up alive!"

The women asked questions for the rest of the day, soaking up stories of Jesus and his friends. Before leaving for the night, they joined hands in prayer, thanking God for Jesus' life and Peter's work.

Then came a morning that is etched in my needle brain like no other. I knew something was terribly wrong. Dorcas had not moved for hours—not even to turn over in her sleep.

But what could I do? I couldn't say a word. I couldn't run for help. If I could have barked like a dog and summoned the neighborhood, I would have. If I could have crawled like a turtle across the floor and down the steps, at least I would have been doing something. But stuck in my little pillow, I was powerless. My needle heart was broken.

Shortly after sunrise the next morning, Dorcas's friends knocked on the door. Hearing no answer, they came in, for the door was always unlocked.

"Where's Dorcas?" said one.

"She must be upstairs already," said another. "She's getting an early start."

"Dorcas, we brought breakfast!"

Footsteps pit-a-patted up the stairs to the flat roof, where the group sewed when the weather was good.

"She's not here!"

"She's sleeping in. Good for her."

Dorcas never slept late.

"I'll check on her," said Priscilla, as she came back down to peek into Dorcas's sleeping nook under the stairs.

"She's not breathing!" Priscilla cried. "She's dead!"

Disbelief filled the house.

"She seemed fine last night!"

As word spread, widows from down the shore raced in, as did those from back alleys and street corners. Soon the home was packed with Dorcas's friends: crying, praying, holding each other in grief.

And then, full of tears, the women prepared their friend for burial. They carried Dorcas to the rooftop, washed her body, brushed her hair, and anointed her with sweet-smelling oil. I was allowed to stay on her wrist in my special pillow. They thought it fitting that she be buried with her best and most trusted tool for doing God's work.

Don't bury me, I thought. *Don't bury Dorcas! We still have work to do!!*

Thank God for Priscilla, who never could stay quiet.

"You know, Jesus brought Lazarus back to life! Maybe Peter can do the same thing for Dorcas!"

What? Bring Dorcas back? Like Lazarus came back after three days of being dead?

"I'll get Gabriel and Michael to run to Lydda!" said Priscilla, disappearing out the door. "Peter must come at once!"

Great idea! Send the young men of the town with their long, fast legs. We knew Michael and Gabriel from Sunday morning worship. Red-haired Michael was as extroverted as the day was long. His brother Gabriel was quieter, but no one spoke more eloquently. If anyone could convince Peter to come, it would be those two.

Slowly the sun climbed in the sky. The women waited and waited. The hours dragged on. Finally the sun went down. Deep, grief-filled cries rose like incense into the sky.

And then, out of the darkness, a massive oak tree of a man appeared in the doorway. It was Peter!

"Save our friend, Peter! Save Dorcas!" cried the women.

"Look at this beautiful coat she made me!" sobbed one woman.

"She keeps us all warm in so many ways!" said another. "We can't live without her!"

"Leave me alone with her!" commanded Peter. "Go outside!"

Silently the women filed out, leaving just the three of us—me and Peter and Dorcas. When the door was shut, Peter knelt down, placing his scarred and callused hands on Dorcas's head.

"Lord God, life and death are in your hands. As you raised Lazarus from the grave, bring this woman back to life...Dorcas, get up!"

At that moment, my old friend's eyes flew open. Color flooded back into her face. Limbs that had been stiff and cold grew warm again! The hands of the rugged fisherman reached for her like an elegant dance partner.

"Come, Dorcas," said Peter. "Stand up."

"But I was...I was..."

"Yes, you were. But God still has work for you to do—right here in Joppa with your friends."

"Then let's get to it," Dorcas said, reaching for me. "Let's get to it."

QUESTIONS TO CONSIDER
YOUNGER READERS

Dorcas and her friends made warm coats for poor women who could not afford them. Have you ever gone to bed hungry or cold? How did that feel?

Describe some ways that you can help others who might not have money to buy good food or warm clothes.

How do you think Dorcas's friends felt when Dorcas came back to life? What would it have been like to be there when that happened?

OLDER READERS

Have you known anyone like Dorcas? What lessons might you learn from Dorcas and others who exhibit such servant ministry?

Dorcas's home was a striking example of an early house church: a place of prayer and companionship with a clearly defined mission of making warm coats for the poor. What can we learn from her leadership?

Aside from the brief story about Dorcas in Acts 9, her ministry goes virtually unnoticed in Christian history. Why do you think that might be?

THE BIBLE STORY

Acts 9:36-42. Now in Joppa there was a disciple whose name was Tabitha, which in Greek is Dorcas. She was devoted to good works and acts of charity. At that time she became ill and died. When they had washed her, they laid her in a room upstairs. Since Lydda was near Joppa, the disciples, who heard that Peter was there, sent two men to him with the request, "Please come to us without delay." So Peter got up and went with them; and when he arrived, they took him to the room upstairs. All the widows stood beside him, weeping and showing tunics and other clothing that Dorcas had made while she was with them. Peter put all of them outside, and then he knelt down and prayed. He turned to the body and said, "Tabitha, get up." Then she opened her eyes, and seeing Peter, she sat up. He gave her his hand and helped her up. Then calling the saints and widows, he showed her to be alive. This became known throughout Joppa, and many believed in the Lord.

ABOUT THE AUTHOR

An Episcopal priest, Lindsay Hardin Freeman has won more than thirty writing awards for journalistic excellence. These stories, originally written for her sons, draw from both a mother's perspective and a deep love for the Bible. *The Spy at Jacob's Ladder* is part of a series of books by Lindsay, including *The Spy on Noah's Ark*. She is also a co-writer for two family storybooks, *The Path* and *Meet the Saints*. She is the author of the award-winning *Bible Women: All Their Words and Why They Matter*, a groundbreaking book that records and explores every word spoken by women in the Bible.

ABOUT THE ARTIST

Paul Shaffer is a freelance illustrator/artist and a retired Episcopal priest who enjoys working with children and youth stories. He is also the illustrator for *The Spy on Noah's Ark* and *Grandpa's Tent,* both with Forward Movement. Paul created the artwork for the Imara International book, *Safe In A Tree*, *Imara and Me*, and the youth guidebooks for the Maiden Spirit and Peace Warriors programs for the Life Blessing Institute. His aim is to continue to develop his art with stories and programs that help children to grow spiritually and emotionally.

ABOUT FORWARD MOVEMENT

Forward Movement is committed to inspiring disciples and empowering evangelists. Our ministry is lived out by creating resources such as books, small-group studies, apps, and conferences. Our daily devotional, *Forward Day by Day*, is also available in Spanish (*Adelante Dia a Dia*) and Braille, online, as a podcast, and as an app for smartphones or tablets. It is mailed to more than fifty countries, and we donate nearly 30,000 copies each quarter to prisons, hospitals, and nursing homes. We actively seek partners across the church and look for ways to provide resources that inspire and challenge. A ministry of the Episcopal Church for over eighty years, Forward Movement is a nonprofit organization funded by sales of resources and by gifts from generous donors.

To learn more about Forward Movement and our resources, visit www.ForwardMovement.org. We are delighted to be doing this work and invite your prayers and support.